Mystical Colors

I0157601

Ori Oasis
OrisOasis.com/OriKids

ISBN-10: 0615948979
ISBN-13: 978-0615948973

NOTE TO PARENTS

My spiritual path has always been a big part of my life. So it was only natural that when I became a mother, I would want to share that part of my life with our children as well. In my search, I have found plenty of beautiful children's books but found it impossible to find one that incorporates spirituality with the basic things a child must learn. I am not saying there aren't any out there but as of yet, they have not crossed my path. So I decided to create my own. Much to my surprise, my family and friends not only loved the idea, but encouraged me to share it with the world. Whether this is the first of its kind, I do not know. My only desire is that after this, more books like these will be readily available for those who seek them.

DEDICATION

To our Ancestral family who paved the way, to our children who are willing to walk that path, and to the family members seeking to aide them on their earthly journey,

Thank You.

ACKNOWLEDGMENTS

To loved ones near and far who are guiding me from the other side,
To the love of my life for always allowing room for my creativity to flourish and grow,
To our boys for always inspiring me to do more,
To my soul sister for helping me expand my dreams further than I could even imagine,
and to all, whether great or small, that have encouraged me in their own way,
Thank you a for being there for me.

Ori

Did you know colors have meanings?
Let's look and see.

Red

Red is the color of strength. What gives you strength?

Yellow

Yellow is the color of joy. What brings you joy?

Pink

Pink is the color of love. Who do you love?

Green

Green is the color of health.
What do you eat to stay healthy?

Purple

Purple is the color of wisdom.
What can you do to gain wisdom?

Orange

Orange is the color of balance.
What can you do to have more balance?

Blue

Blue is the color of peace.
What brings you peace?

White

White is the color of youth. How young are you?

Black

Black is the color of mystery.
What mysterious things do you want to
learn about?

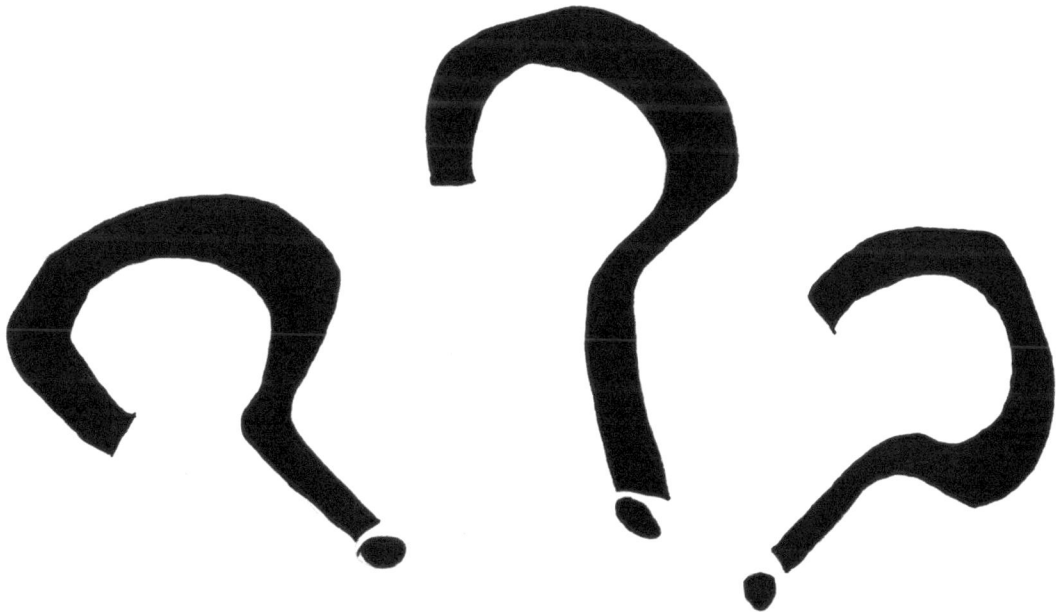

Brown

Brown is the color of earth.
How many flowers can you name?

I love learning the meanings of colors.
How about you?

ABOUT THE AUTHOR

Nothing is ever happenstance and this life was brought to me because we asked for each other.

As well as being a wife and mother, I am the owner and creator of Ori Oasis and OrisOasis.com. For over twelve years, I have done Astrology readings, channeling, oracle readings, as well as being a mentor to others.

www.ingramcontent.com/pod-product-compliance
Lightning Source LLC
Chambersburg PA
CBHW042105040426
42448CB00002B/142